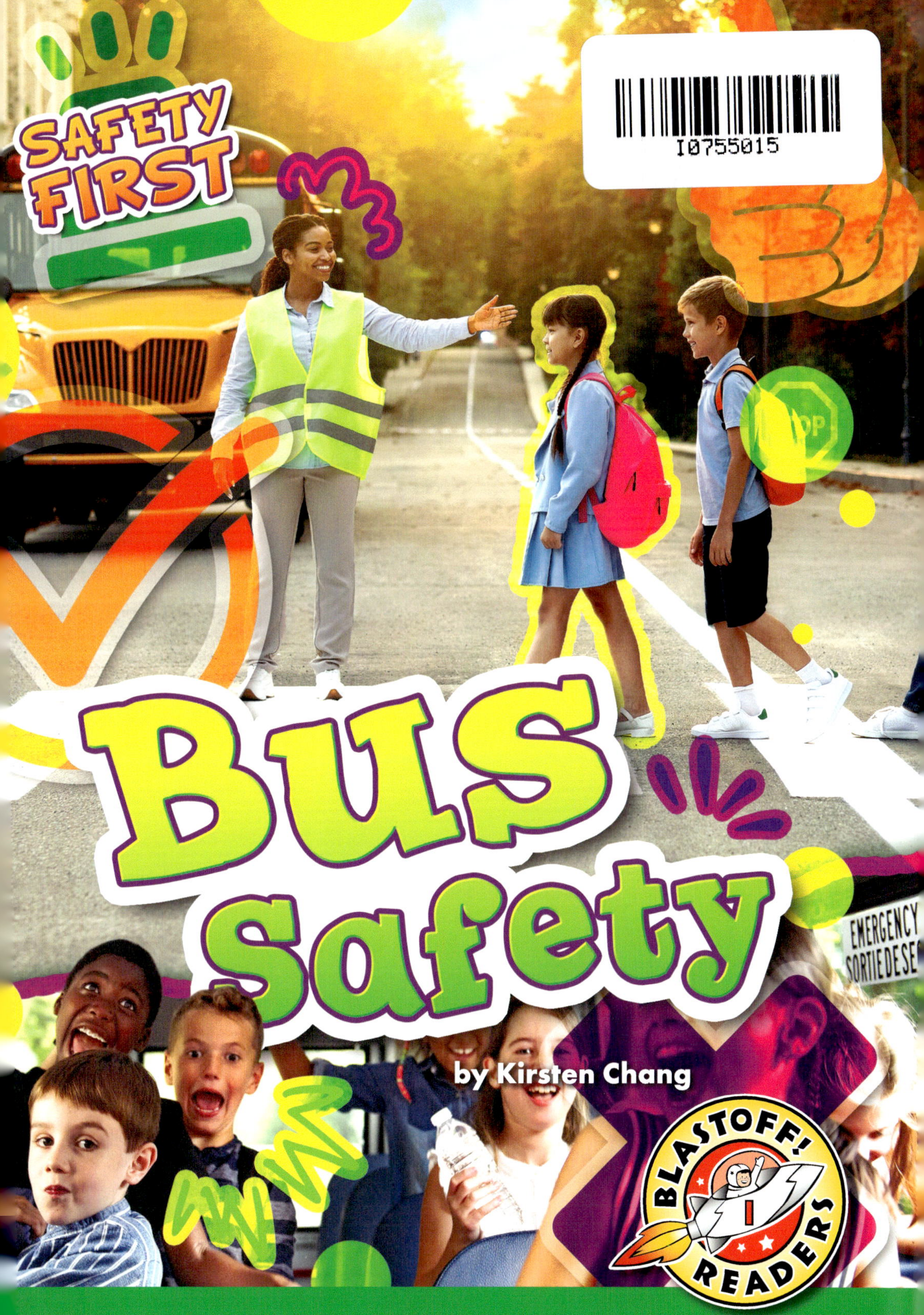




# Bus Safety

by Kirsten Chang

BLASTOFF! READERS

BLASTOFF! READERS, AN IMPRINT OF BELLWETHER MEDIA BY FLUTTERBEE

**Blastoff! Readers** are carefully developed by literacy experts to build reading stamina and move students toward fluency by combining standards-based content with developmentally appropriate text.

**Level 1** provides the most support through repetition of high-frequency words, light text, predictable sentence patterns, and strong visual support.

**Level 2** offers early readers a bit more challenge through varied sentences, increased text load, and text-supportive special features.

**Level 3** advances early-fluent readers toward fluency through increased text load, less reliance on photos, advancing concepts, longer sentences, and more complex special features.

★ **Blastoff! Universe**

Reading Level

Grade K

Grades 1–3

Grade 4

This edition first published in 2027 by Bellwether Media, Inc.



For information regarding permission, write to Bellwether Media, Inc., Attention: Permissions Department, 3500 American Blvd W, Suite 150, Bloomington, MN 55431.

Library of Congress Cataloging-in-Publication Data is available at www.loc.gov or upon request from the publisher.

ISBN: 9798898800352 (hardcover)
ISBN: 9798898802882 (paperback)
ISBN: 9798898801595 (ebook)

Editor: Rachael Barnes    Designer: Andrea Schneider

Printed in the United States of America, North Mankato, MN.

# Table of Contents

## Riding Safely

Liam rides the bus. The bus takes many kids to school!

## Why Stay Safe?

Buses are large **vehicles**. We are **cautious** around them. Can the driver see us?

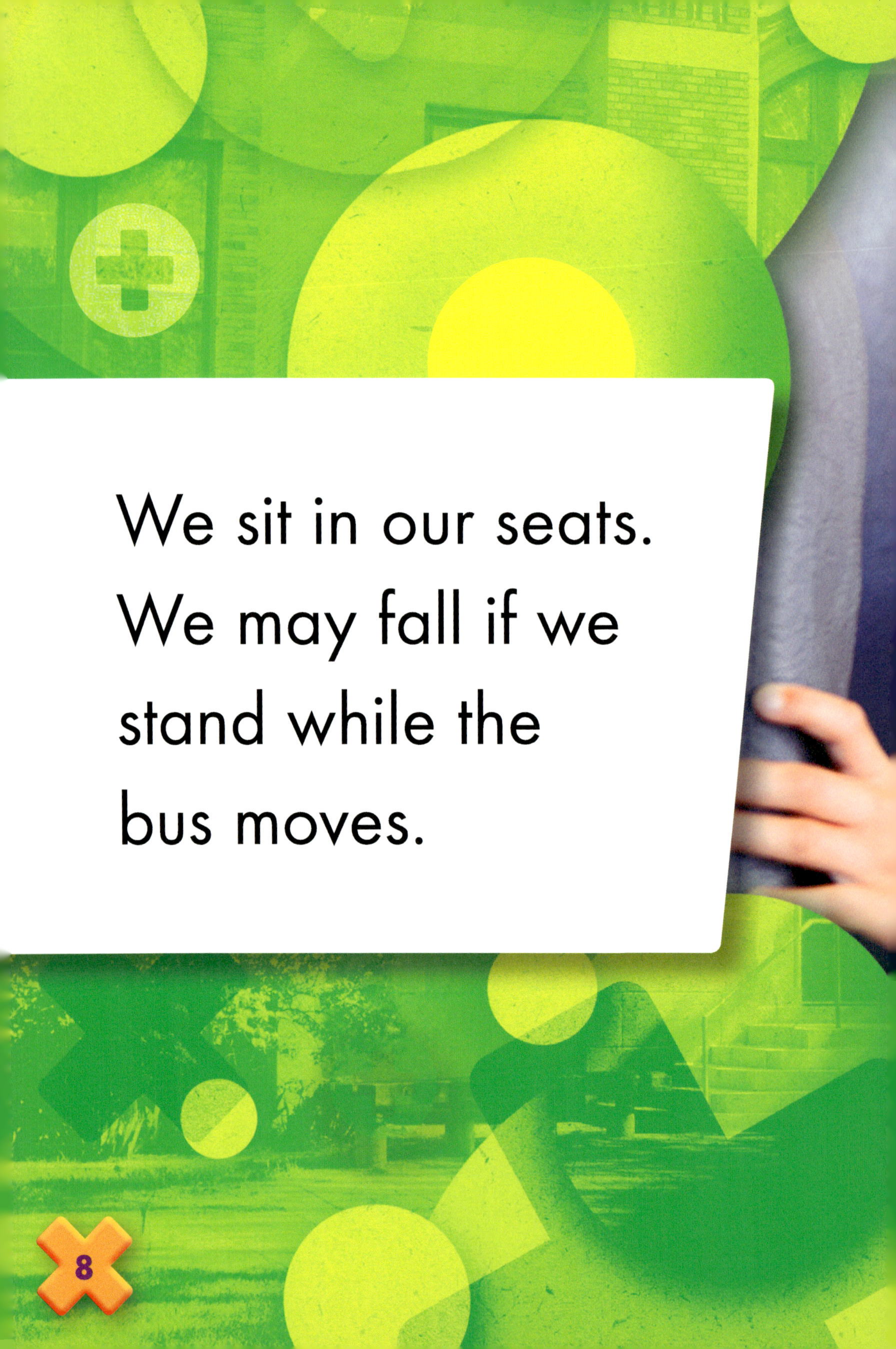

We sit in our seats. We may fall if we stand while the bus moves.

We talk quietly. Noise **distracts** the driver. People can get hurt.

Safety Rules
STOP
Wait five steps behind the curb.
Wait for the bus to stop completely.
Sit in your seat and face forward.
Talk quietly.

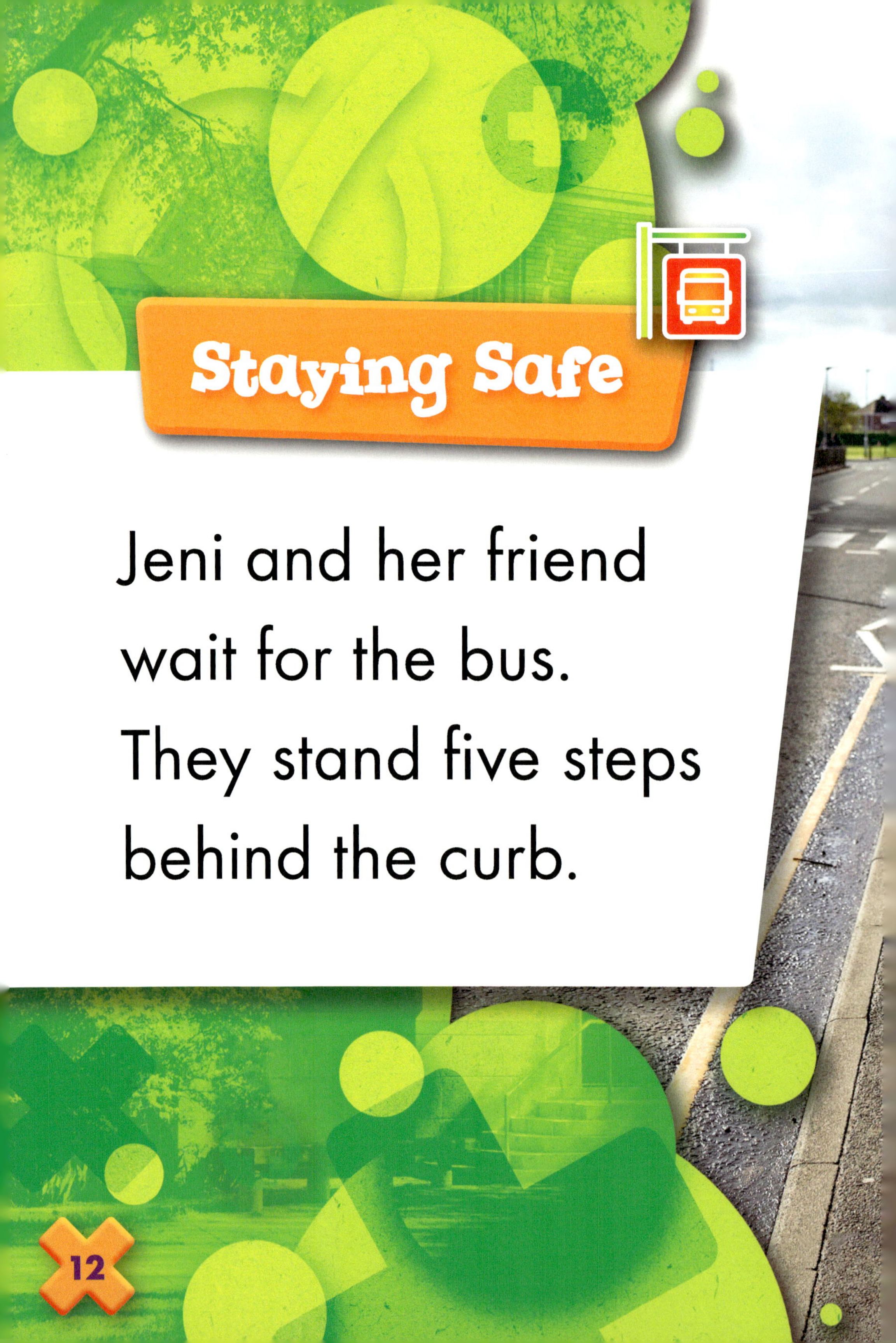

# Staying Safe

Jeni and her friend wait for the bus. They stand five steps behind the curb.

The bus stops completely. The driver opens the door. AJ can **board** now!

driver

We sit in our seats
and face forward.
We use inside voices.

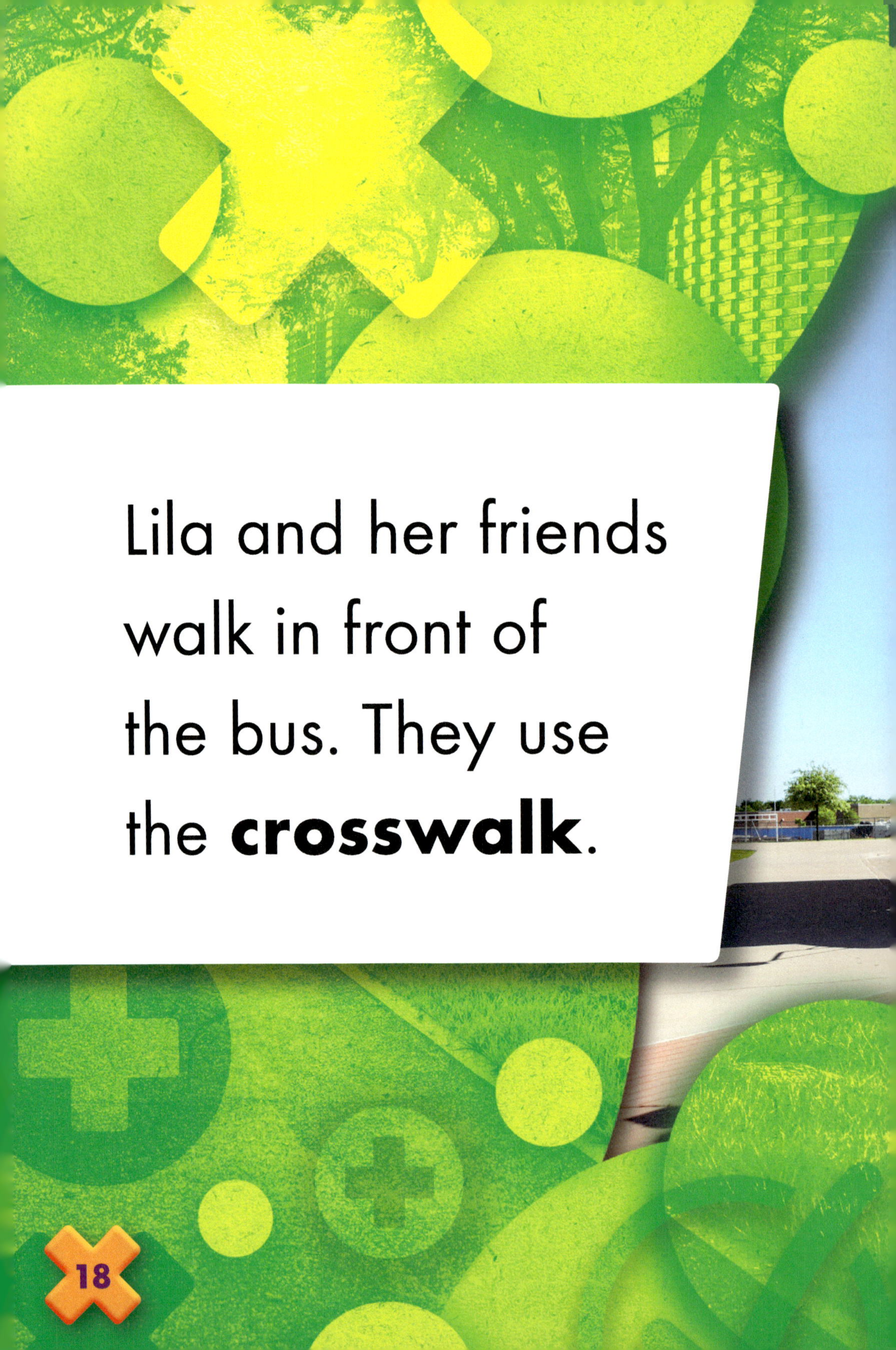

Lila and her friends walk in front of the bus. They use the **crosswalk**.

# How to Exit the Bus

**Exit** the bus **calmly.**

**Never walk behind** the bus.

Take **five big steps** past the front of the bus.

**Look both ways** before crossing the street.

crosswalk

Dad waits at the bus stop. Jess got home safely!

# Glossary

**board**

to get on

**cautious**

careful

**crosswalk**

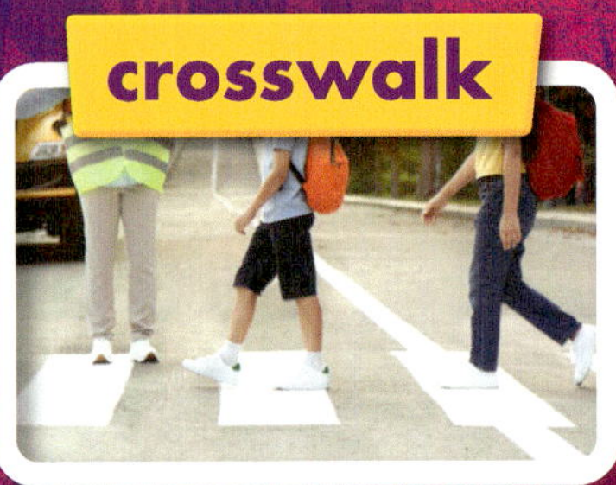

a specially marked place to cross a street

**distracts**

takes someone's attention away from something

**vehicles**

machines that take people from one place to another

# To Learn More

## AT THE LIBRARY

Bassier, Emma. *Bus Safety*. Minneapolis, Minn.: Pop!, 2021.

Gates, Margo. *The School Bus*. Minneapolis, Minn.: Lerner Publications, 2023.

Toolen, Avery. *A Day with a Bus Driver*. Minneapolis, Minn.: Jump!, 2022.

## ON THE WEB

**FACTSURFER**

Factsurfer.com gives you a safe, fun way to find more information.

1. Go to www.factsurfer.com.
2. Enter "bus safety" into the search box and click 🔍.
3. Select your book cover to see a list of related content.

# Index

The images in this book are reproduced through the courtesy of: Prostock-studio, front cover (top), p. 22 (crosswalk); lisegagne, front cover (bottom), p. 22 (distracts); Claudio Divizia, p. 3 (sign); Roxana, p. 3 (bus); Jaren Wicklund, pp. 4-5; Stuart Monk, pp. 6-7; SDI Productions, pp. 8-9, 14-15, 16-17, 18-19; oneinchpunch, p. 9 (inset); FatCamera, pp. 10-11, 20-21; dglimages, pp. 12-13; martinedoucet, p. 22 (board); JenkoAtaman, p. 22 (cautious); David Prahl, p. 22 (vehicles); kromkrathog, p. 23.